POETIC
LOVE LETTERS
& More

DONNIE JACKSON

POETIC LOVE LETTERS & MORE
Copyright © 2024   Donnie Jackson

All rights reserved. No part of this book may be used or reproduced by any means, graphic, electronic, or mechanical, including photocopying, recording, taping or by any information storage retrieval system without the written permission of the author except in the case of brief quotations embodied in critical articles and reviews.

Because of the dynamic nature of the Internet, any web addresses or links contained in this book may have changed since publication and may no longer be valid. The views expressed in this work are solely those of the author and do not necessarily reflect the views of the publisher, and the publisher hereby disclaims any responsibility for them.

Library of Congress Control Number:	2024944870
Paperback:	979-8-89306-079-9
eBook:	979-8-89306-080-5

Printed in the United States of America

Table of Contents

Forward .... *v*
Acknowledgements .... *vii*
Dedication .... *ix*
A Tribute to My Father 1
A Friend Like you 3
Admirations 5
Blind Obsession 7
Broken 9
Burning With Desire 11
Darlene 13
Changing Times 15
Deception 17
Empty Promises 19
Forbidden Love 21
Happy Birthday! 23
Friends To The End 25
Doubt and Fear 27
Is This Love 29
Is She The One? 31
I Miss You! 33
If I Was Free 35
It's Just A Dream 37
It's Not Funny 39
Life" 41
Just One Kiss 43
Love Conquers All 45
Memories 47
Missed Opportunity? 49
My Gift for You 51
My Heart's Letter 53

My Love No Longer Call	55
My Shelter in the Time of Storms	57
Never Say Never	59
No Love in My Heart	61
No More Tears	63
One way Love Affair	65
Prisoner of Love	67
Rejected	69
Sad Goodbye	71
"She"	73
Smooth Seduction	75
Someone Who Cares	77
Tanya	79
The Ultimate Love	81
This Too Shall Pass	83
Where We Belong	85
Who Is She	87
About the Author	89

Forward

First of all, I want to take this time to give honor and praise to Yahweh, and to my Savior Yahushua ha'Mashiah. Poetic Love Letters & More is a collection of poems that are mostly based on my personal experiences, as well as influences from close friends. Some of whom I have never actually met, but only knew through internet, and phone correspondence. The poems display a lot of emotions which take you from happy, to sad, and all points between. Some of them also touch on current issues that we face in our daily lives. Issues such as teen pregnancy, gay marriage, love, heartache, heart break, and the list goes on.

Within the pages of this book you are sure to read something that will grab you in some way. You may even read something that describes your own situation, something you yourself is going through, or the situation of someone you know. Many of the poems that deal with love are inspired by personal experiences that I have had or that of friends. Consider the poem "Burning with Desire," which contains 99% of the words of a friend of mine whom I only speak to over the phone but who nevertheless displays a burning desire to be with me. The poem "No Love in My Heart" was inspired by a friend of mine who told me she has no love in her heart. I wrote the poem "This Too Shall Pass" in support of a close friend who was going through a very difficult time. Many people who read or heard the poem found comfort in it.

My hope is that when you read these poems you will enjoy them and tell your friends and family about them. I want to thank you in advance for your support. May Yahweh bless you, your family, and your friends for the rest of your days!

Donnie Jackson

Acknowledgements

First, I want to thank my wife Charlotte Jackson for always standing by me in spite of all the pain and heartaches I caused. You have been the best wife any man could ever ask for and I surely do not deserve you! Next, I want to thank my family, my mother Hannah Jackson, my sisters Connie, Sheila, Beverly, Carmen, and Patricia, and my only brother Isaac. Thank you all for your love and support.

I would also like to acknowledge a few people who have inspired some of my poems such as Lavern Williams, Roshell Morgan, Melinda Smith, Loretta Howard, Kimberly Smichowski, and Brenda Morales. All of whom contributed to this project in some way. Thank you all!

Dedication

I dedicate this book to my father Arthur Jackson. At the time this book was written he was suffering with terminal cancer, which ended up taking his life. He was the strongest man I knew, but I don't mean physical strength, I'm talking about emotional strength. I watch Pop go through many adverse situations, but nothing ever shakes him, he is always even keel. You can never tell when he is going through a tough situation because he never shows any emotion.

Pop I know I never told you enough, but "I love you" very much!

A Tribute to My Father
For his 80th birthday

Pop today we're celebrating your 80th birthday
And it's on your request why we're doing it this way

You have been through a lot in these recent years
But never once have I ever seen you crying any tears

As a father you have been there throughout my whole life
I was only four, when you made mom your wife

I've watched you struggle, trying to make two ends meet
Carrying two heavy shrimp's buckets, and never missed a beat

You've been a tailor, a steel worker, and you work in the field
You played dominoes for milk, but never have you steal

Donnie Jackson

You were always firm with us, whenever we got out of line
And it didn't mean you never loved us when you wale our behind

So pop I want to thank you, for the way that you raise me
And I hope when you look at me, you are proud of what you see

You raised seven of us, and we all turned out fine
You even raised you grandchildren, but none of them were mine

A Friend Like You

A true friend will stand with you through thick and thin
If you are in a fire and call out, they'll quickly run in

Whenever I think of a true friend, I always think of you
You are the kind of friend who is always there, and I can always turn to

No matter the time, weather night or day
Whenever I call, you are on your way

If I make a mistake you don't find faults or judge
And if I do you wrong, you don't hold a grudge

Friends like you are truly a rare find
Friends like you are truly one of a kind

So I wanna take this time for just a minute or two
To let you know I am very lucky, to have a friend like you

Admirations

Once again I am inspired
To write about things that I truly admired

Like how so many go through life without ever knowing love
Yet it is freely given to everyone, by the Creator up above

I think about the mystery of the day, how it always changes to night
And even when you don't see the sun, the day is always light

I look out of my window, and watch the snow fall
And I think of all the oak trees, how they grow so tall

I admire all the nice homes, and all the fancy cars
Not to mention all the planets, and also the billions of stars

What make the storm clouds pour out the rain?
And why when your heart breaks, you feel no physical pain

You have to admit, it is fascinating to see a mother giving birth
And think about all the different people, who are living on the earth

We all need food and water, it's the only way we survive
Yet if we didn't have air to breathe, we would not be alive

It is a marvelous thing indeed, how we can always gain more knowledge
When we do our best in school, and then later go to college

I admire those who will stand up, to defend the rights of another
I admire the single mothers, who raise their kids without a fathers

I can go on and on talking about this, but I'm sure you got the idea
That in this marvelous world we live in, there are so much that we can admire

Blind Obsession

People are truly a very peculiar being
They can develop strong feelings for others they've never seen

Ignoring those in need whom they seen everyday
Not letting the plight of others affect them in anyway

People these days are so superficial
They will look at one's picture and determine they are special

Not knowing if that person is either good or bad
Or if their demeanor is either happy or sad

They can fall in love with someone they may never even meet
Someone they saw in passing as they are walking down the street

Then they decided in their heart that together they belong
Thus began the endless journey of a love affair of one

Trying hard every day to make a good impression
Hoping no one will ever know about your blind obsession

Broken

Oh how I wish that I were dead
If it were not a sin I'd put a bullet through my head

My life is so miserable I just cannot take it
Why can't I truly be happy, and not just fake it

I made a decision years ago which I felt I had no choice
Now all these years later, it is time to pay the price

Trying to do the right thing that was expected of me
Now I find myself in a place where I do not want to be

From that one decision, three lives were affected

And I ruin the lives of two, so that one would be protected

If only I have a chance to do it over again
Based on what I know now that I did not knew then

I am so torn up inside, there are no words to be spoken
But if I had to describe how I feel, I'd simply say; I am broken

Burning With Desire

Burning with desire
My body is on fire

Though my eyes have never beheld you
My body yearns desperately for you

And the sound of your voice is like an aphrodisiac
How I long for the moment when we make eye contact

When at last our lips will finally meet
And I savor the taste of your kisses so sweet

A frequent visitor in my dream
You feel so real you make me scream

The desire is so strong, and the want is so much
What wouldn't I do just to feel your touch!

I'm going insane and I don't understand
Never have I felt this way about anyone

I cannot concentrate on nothing that I do
My mind is totally consumed with thoughts of making love to you

How can this feel so right, when inside I know it's wrong?
Why do I want you so badly when there's another to whom you belong?

Darlene

Darlene oh Darlene, why act like a damsel when you are a queen
Why let your past turn someone so sweet into someone so mean

The men in your life have not been the best
But don't give up yet, you have not tried the rest

You have proven that you are a true survivor
You are not just some old lady Godiva

You deserve honor, love, and respect
And if you persevere, that you will surely get

You've been on your own for a very long time
And yet your kids turned out just fine

You've seen many changes, and even menopause
So don't give up now, stand up for your cause

In a year and two days you will be forty seven
This means you are getting much closer to heaven

But until then your life you still have to live
And I'm sure in your heart, you have more love to give

Changing Times

So many things have changed since time has begun
It is so much different now from when we were young

Things that once hold value to us
Today sits around just gathering dust

And our moral values are in such decay
You scratch your head and wonder how it got that way

Babies having babies at a rapid pace
And no one seems to think it is a big disgrace

You have men changing to women, and women changing to men
And same sex marriage once unheard of, now happens again and again

In the past such things could never be
And those old enough, I'm sure will agree

But we are living in changing times, nothing stays the same
Children have no respect for their elders, and you wonder who is to blame

Some blame the parents for not having stricter rules
Others blame society, some even blame the schools

But no matter who you blame, these are changing times
So it is very important that whatever we do, we always develop our minds

Deception

What do you do when you know you are lying?
You pretend you are happy but inside you are dying

When the one you are with has been so good to you
But you are in love with another and don't know what to do

It is a very hard decision that you have to make
When for you to be happy, someone's heart you must break

You have to ask yourself; what will you really gain?
When the decision you must make will cause so much pain

Do you go on living the lie, hoping it will work out for all?
Or do you make the tough decision, and let the chips lie where they fall

One thing is for certain, there is no easy solution
And like it or not, you'll have to come to a conclusion

But when it is all said and done, will you be happy indeed
Because no matter how bad you want it, happiness is not guaranteed

Empty Promises

Have you ever had an idea that you think was so great
So much so, that to make it a reality, you can hardly wait

Have you ever had something that you wanted badly to do
But to accomplish your task, it depends on more than just you

It is a frustrating situation, that you hate to be in
Because without the help of others, you cannot begin

So you share your idea with everyone who will listen
And though the responses are good, there is still something missing

I got an idea and wrote the lyrics for a song
Now if I can only add music, everyone could sing along

But I am not a musician, and I can't play a note
So what will become of this song that I wrote?

I went to someone who I know is a musician
I told him about my song, and explain my possession

He said I love your idea; I will make sure that it flourishes
But in the end it was just talk, it was only empty promises

Forbidden Love

We started out so innocently
Now we share a love that should never be

You see my dear, this love we share
Although it's so strong, I can feel that it's wrong

And my mind tells me that you might understand
When I tell you my love, we cannot go on

My love for you will never grow cold
Your precious memories will comfort my soul

But my heart cries out, and I must change my life
No more cheating or misleading, no more lying to me wife

The time has come for me to settle down
Got to change my ways, no more running around

Got to give up my lies, and all my alibis
And all the things I do, which brings tears to her eyes

I make many friends wherever I go
Throughout the US, and in Mexico

Some of them I see on a regular basis
Different creed, different color, and different races

I left broken hearts here and there
And when I think about it, it's just not fair

So I guess what I am telling you is goodbye
And I pray you'll understand, and you will not cry

You must find your happiness in the one up above
For there is only disappointment, in our forbidden love

Happy Birthday

Happy Birthday! Today is the day you aged a whole year
It is time to celebrate, get something special to wear
Get a new pair of shoes, do something nice with your hair
Tonight you celebrate like you just don't care

Some will say you're getting older, but you're actually getting better
You're another year older which means you are also getting wiser
You no longer do some of the things that you did when you were younger
And the only thing that changes in your age is just the number

So today is a day for you to let it all go
Be spontaneous, have some fun, just go with the flow
You can lay back, take some time for yourself and just take it slow
Or go out with a bunch of friends and see a Broadway show

But whatever you do today make sure it is all about you
You should only do things today that you want to do
Be sure that you are not influenced by your friends or your family too
No matter what they say or do, to yourself you must remain true
Happy Birthday! from me to you!

Friends To The End

We've been friends since we were young, and that's a very long time
And if we were only allowed just one friend, I'd be yours, and you'd be mine

We grow up together in our early age
But like reading a book, you have to turn the page

And as time goes by we would drift apart
But we always kept each other inside our hearts

We've seen friends come, and we saw them go
But we stay together, no matter where the wind blow

We have a special bond, that is like none other
We were not only good friends, but we were also lovers

We share lots of good times, and some bad times too
But in spite of it all, our friendship remains true

I have no regrets from the time we met, I am proud to say you're my friend
I hope that nothing will ever chance, and we'll remain friends to the end

Doubt and Fear

Two of the biggest enemies in our lives are doubt and fear
They are always ready to prevent you from moving free and clear

Whenever you have an opportunity to start branching out
And especially if there's some risk involved; here comes doubt

That dirty rotten scoundrel, starts to whisper in your ear
And if you ever try to resist him, he then teams up with fear

If you're not careful, they will surely overpower you
But you have to know that there's a power, greater, inside you

So don't let these two jokers play you like a toy
They are just thieves and robbers, trying to steal your joy

Sometimes the risk is great, but the reward is greater
And you only have now to act, sometimes there is no later

The enemy likes to keep you in the dark and out of the light
But remember, we walk by faith, and not by sight

So never let doubt and fear ever creep inside your head
They just want to take your joy, and give you sorrow instead

Is This Love

What is love, does anyone even know
How do I learn about it, is there some place that I can go?

Can you know love by the way that you feel?
And how can you know if what you feel is even real

When you see someone who makes your heart starts to race
Then you make eye contact which brings a smile to your face
Is that love?

I met someone one day and I felt a real connection
We have so many things in common, there was no room for rejection

We spend countless hours in loving conversation
Saying things to each other we never said to anyone

We share a love that was so strong, we never wanted it to end
So we made a promise that a life without each other we never wanted to spend

But then one day, I said something I never should have said
It's like I drove a spear through her heart, now the love we share is dead

But although I may no longer be in her heart, she'll remain always in mine
The only way she will not be in my heart, is if the sun no longer shines

Is She The One

What has she done to me?
Why is she the only one that I see?
Could she really be the one for me?
Of these thing I do wonder

Girls in my life there has been many
Five, ten, fifteen, twenty
But compare to her there is not any
She brings me great joy, and makes my heart grow fonder

Is she the one who will ease my pain?
And gives me shelter from the pouring rain
Or is she a love that will end in vain
These things in my heart I do ponder

But for now I will enjoy her warm embrace
And the wonderful smile she puts on my face
And if she is the one, no time, we will waste
I will make her my goose, and I will be her gander

I Miss You

Oh how I miss you, let me count the ways
Since the last time that I saw you, there has been far too many days

I'm so miserable without you, baby can't you see?
How long will you continue to withhold your love from me?

Oh how I am missing you so very much
My body keeps on yearning for the tenderness of your touch

The way that you would hold me, and the sweet things you say
How could it be that our love end up this way?

My heart is slowly dying, and you alone holds the cure
The pain is so overwhelming, I can't take it anymore

Baby I truly miss you, and I know you miss me too
Not talking to you or seeing you, has left me oh so blue
I miss you baby!

If I Was Free

Oh if only I was free
Free to be what I wanted to be
To travel the world, there's so much to see
If only there was no one depending on me

I could be spontaneous and just go with the flow
At the drop of a hat I could get up and go
I could let the wind take me wherever it blow
And where I would end up, who would ever know

It is a wonderful dream but in reality
There are so many people depending on me
So many places that I have to be
And so many people who want to see me

It's Just A Dream

Woke up this morning and got a scare
I look beside me, and you were not there
I started searching everywhere
But could not find you anywhere

I thought I lost you, so it seems
I search the valleys, rivers, and streams
And just as I was about to scream
I woke up and realize, it's just a dream

It's Not Funny

It's not funny
The way you make me feel
It's not funny
This feeling is for real
It's not funny
When you play me like a toy
It's not funny
Even though you bring me joy
It's not funny
Because the joy could soon be sorrow
It's not funny
Knowing you could be gone tomorrow

Life

Life is a gift worth living
Love is a gift worth giving
Love is the key to peace
Peace is the key to happiness
Happiness in Yahushua
That's the key to life

Just One Kiss

Just one kiss was all it took
Now our lives has become an open book

Feelings that we've kept hidden inside
Is now on display, no more can we hide

We release emotions that we thought was dead
Now when we are around each other we want to be in bed

Who would ever think that just one kiss
Would spark a love affair as wonderful as this

We've known each other for such a long time
Yet we never thought I would be yours, and you'd be mine

But at that magical moment on a cool autumn night
We embrace each other, and it felt so right

Donnie Jackson

Then just one kiss, sets it all in motion
It was like taking a drink of a strong love potion

You intoxicate me, and I could not resist
I just had to have it, just one kiss

Love Conquers All

When it seems like our love would never be
It was just a testimony for all to see

That despite the obstacles in our way
Our love persevered day by day

And those who would want to see us fail
Watch our love breaks new ground and blaze new trail

Our love has truly stood the test of time
It went through the fire and came out refine

And no matter how many times we rise and fall
One thing stays true, love conquers all

Memories

Memories: how do you make them go away?
No matter how hard I try, they always want to stay

The good ones make me smile, so they I don't mind
But the bad one that makes me angry, comes back all the time

Why can't they just go away like the ones who create them do?
It should be a rule that when you leave, your memories goes with you

But instead they just hung around for no good reason
Except to bring joy and pain, at any time, in any season

So help me find a way to make these memories go away
You can charge me whatever you like, I will gladly pay

Missed Opportunity

We were once so very close a very long time ago
But we were so very young, how were we to know
That the love we once share if given a chance it would grow
Would we be together today, that we will never know!

We live separate lives, and as a result we grew apart
But we always have each other deep inside our hearts
Now the feelings we once had is again aroused in our thoughts
And although we want to be together, they are reasons we should not start

So for now we will just reflect on the memories that we've share
Of a time way back in our past when we didn't have a care
Not about what we would eat, or even what we would wear
And the only times that matters to us, were the times when we were near

But things and times have change, and we are no longer the same
And although we want to play again, we realize it's not a game
I have since gotten married, and you also did the very same
But if we were meant for each other, wouldn't that just be a shame!

My Gift for You

I have a special gift for you
No courier I can send it through
It's not a gift that one can steal
But one you can definitely feel

It can't be wrapped up in paper, or tied up with a bow
But it can make you sparkle, maybe even glow
It is shared by many throughout the world
And it is worth more than diamonds, and more than pearl

Some have died for it, others kill for it, so many stories been told
When you have it, the world is a happy place, but without it, it's so cold
When you get it, you have to share it, or it will be of no use to you
It's even better, and much more special, when it is shared by two

This gift I have is so unique, it can travel through time and space
It is so diverse, and so adaptable; it transcends all culture and race
My gift for you is so very special, it was sent from Heaven above
You see my gift is warm and true, my gift for you, is love

My Heart's Letter

I try to resist
But my heart kept insist

That I write you this letter
Said it will make me feel better

So I reach for my pad, and I pick up my pen
But I could not decide just how to begin

I can say that I love you, and you know that it's true
Or even that I miss you, and longing to hold you

But no matter what I say, or anything that I do
Nothing can ever change the things that you and I been through

So I'll say what I've said right from the start
Only you, and you alone, holds the key to my heart

My Love No Longer Call

I waited and I listen
But something sure was missing

It was that all familiar sound
Of your very special ring tone

You suddenly stops calling
Now the tears won't stop falling

Why did you go away?
What did I do, what did I say

You said our love was true
But you left me sad and blue

So, now I sit alone and stare at the wall
Wondering why my love no longer call

My Shelter in the Time of Storms

Yahweh, I thank You, because You never fail
I thank You Father, because in all things You prevail

When I look at all the things that You do
It gives me great comfort knowing I can always count on You

You said You will never leave me, or will You forsake me
And You have a mansion prepared for me

Though I don't always do the thing that is right
You said I am always precious in Your sight

You gave me Your word to keep me on the right path
Men judge me by my appearance, but You look at my heart

So, thank you Father, for accepting me with open arms
Father I thank you, for always being my shelter in the storms

Never Say Never

So many images going around in my head
I often reflect on some of the things that you said
And the times we spent relaxing in your bed
Now I have to wonder, where has it all lead?

Oh how I am missing you so very much
Your smile, your kiss, your love, your touch
Your tender memories that gives me a rush
How could it be that our love end as such?

Never has anyone made me feel this way before
A love so intoxicating, I just wanted more and more
I miss all those times we went for walks at the shore
And even the times I went with you to the store

Our love was so strong, I never thought it could be severed
And if anyone ever asks me, I would say it was for ever
But it just goes to show, that nothing last forever
It doesn't matter how safe it looks, you can never say never

No Love in My Heart

I tried with love so many times
But it always seems to leave me behind

Just when I think everything is going fine
Love never fails to just blow my mind

It always started out much the same way
First a look, then a smile, then talking everyday

And just when I get to where I can't do without it
That is always the point when love wants to quit

So I'm tired of love keeps tearing me apart
I am through with it, there's no love in my heart

No More Tears

I hung up the phone and I ask myself why
Why do I allow you to always make me cry?

Never in my life have I ever cried so many tears
No one ever affect me like this in all my many years

This love that we share is so very strong
And in our hearts, we know that together we belong

Whenever we get a chance to spend some time together
Our hearts are warm and fuzzy, no matter what the weather

But our love is not without its share of adversity
We are not free to be the way we would like it to be

So at the first sight of resistance, you opt to rip us apart
Thus driving another spear straight through my heart

But I cried so many times throughout the last year
I cannot cry anymore, there's just no more tears

One way Love Affair

What do you do when you are with someone most of your life?
And you try to be the best husband, or be the best wife

Doing everything you can, to fulfill their every need
While working hard day and night, trying to make sure you succeed

But the one you are with doesn't feel the same
They keep breaking your heart and causing you pain

Still you remain ever faithful, and you stay on your course
Because you don't want your marriage ending up in divorce

You fell in love with your spouse, and gave them your heart
And in your vows you say the words until death do us part

So you forgive them, every time that they've done you wrong
Hoping one day they'll realize that with you is where they belong

But the more you show them love, hoping for a little in return
It seems the only love you get is the kind of love that burn

And when you think you faced all the obstacles that you will ever see
You find out they're in love with another, and that's where they want to be

So you think of all the pain you suffered, and all the wasted years
Trying to make a successful marriage from a one way love affair

Now you are faced with a dilemma, in a place you don't want to be
Because you know when your spouse looks at you, it's not you they want to see

Prisoner of Love

I was caught and arrested
Tried and convicted

You captured me with your smile
Not to mention your elegant style

And the gentleness of your touch
Makes me want you oh so much

You're like an ancient treasure that one find
But forbidden to take and have to leave behind

Now my time is spent all day through
Trying to think of ways to spend time with you

And no matter how I try I just can't break free
From this captivating spell that you cast on me

You are an angel who came down from above
Just to make me a prisoner of love

Rejected

Casually browsing online I came across your profile
Immediately I was captured by your captivating smile
I sent you a friend request, and you accepted after a while
And after talking to you I realize that I really like your style

The more we talk the closer we got, and it became very clear to me
That maybe there is something else here, and if so, I would like to see
I told you of what I was thinking, and I was happy that you agree
So we arrange to meet each other, and we decided on where it should be

Now the time has come when we will meet, and I got so very excited
Just the thought of me seeing you made my heart so very delighted
Never was there another occasion, that was so much anticipated
But it was all for naught because you never showed, then I realized, I was rejected

Sad Goodbye

I took you to the airport and I kiss you goodbye
I was so sad on my way home, tears welled up in my eye
I was so overwhelmed that I broke down and I cry
I could not understand I had to ask myself why

Why am I so sad, you'll only be gone for a few days
But for the sweet love you give me, there's a price I must pay
I think how I will miss you; then I started to count the ways
How you hold me and caress me, and the sweet things you would say

But then I think of how nice it will be
When Yahweh once again brings you back to me
When you walk out that terminal, and your sweet face I'll see
And you're back in my arms again, where you always will be

She

She came out of no where
And suddenly she was there

She makes her residence in my heart
And totally dominates all of my thoughts

She is a delicate flower
Who stands strong like a tower

She has beauty and grace
And a radiant smile upon her face

She is every man's dreams
Yet she is mine, so it seems

Could this really be so?
Please tell me, I'd like to know

Could this really be my chance?
At that one special dance

As we drift away together
Sharing our love with each other

Smooth Seduction

I saw you watching me from way across the room
Then I thought to myself, there is a bright spot in all the gloom

I started hoping you would come my way
But if you did come, what would I say

You look so confident, it is almost intimidating
But the thought of being with you, is oh so exhilarating

My heart starts beating fast as I slowly walk towards you
And then it started thumping as you approach me too

We came together and it was magical
I knew right then I would need a sabbatical

I was embarking on a journey that's gonna take some time
And the way that you seduced me, should really be a crime

I didn't know what I was in for, but I knew it would be great
I could tell that my time with you would be no ordinary date

You took me to your apartment, and you put on quite a show
Then you say make love to me, but do it nice and slow

Someone Who Cares

What's happening to me?
It is like I am looking but I just cannot see
And I am miles away from where I should be
How will I find my way, can someone help me?

I went on a journey which for years I anticipate
I just knew when I got there everything would be great
I was so very excited, I just could not wait
But when I finally got there, I was much too late

This cannot be happening, I've waited for years
To enjoy much happiness, and lots of good cheers
But instead I am broken, and fighting back tears
And hoping that somewhere, there is someone who cares

Tanya

Tonya oh Tanya; How is it that you are a nurse
Yet since I met you, I've only gotten worst

Wanting so badly to hear from you
Is like having a severe case of swine flu

And there is no other remedy for me I'm sure
Because it is only you who holds the cure

All that's required for me to feel better
Is just a simple hello in a note or a letter

Patiently I am waiting, just to hear from you
Checking every day, for just a word or two

So I hope this poem will help you to see
What being your friend really means to me

The Ultimate Love

Have you ever loved and lost
Standing at the foot of the cross
You have a choice between the one you love
And the one who is known as the Ultimate love

The one you love is passionate to the core
But the Ultimate love is all that and much more
So a war rage on between your flesh and your spirit
Because your flesh wants your lover, but your spirit isn't in it

You see, the one who you love is temporal
But the Ultimate love is everlasting, and eternal
So it is time for you to make a decision
And you know you have to make the right one

Do you choose a life of pleasures with the one who you love?
Or a life you can treasure with the Ultimate love
The choice is so clear even a blind man can see
I choose the Ultimate love, which last for eternity

This Too Shall Pass

You live and you learn
And you hope you don't get burn

But on the journey we call life
You suffer conflicts, and you suffer strife

You will often make choices that you wish that you could change
But life is not some project you can go back and rearrange

When the decision that you make is so good that it makes you proud
You don't mind if people are talking, let them shout it out loud

But when you make a bad decision which ends up causing you some shame
It makes you wish that you were somewhere where nobody knows your name

Though life can bring you joy, it can also bring you sorrow
And those who slander you today, will be the ones being slandered tomorrow

I know it's no consolation, but I say be not dismay
Because the world will keep on turning, and every dog will have their day

You may be hurting deep inside right now, but the pain will never last
Because the word of Elohim clearly states; this too my friend, will pass

Where We Belong

I've searched for you throughout my whole life
You are the one who will be my wife

And now that I found you, I won't let you go
But I won't move too fast, I will take it real slow

My heart says I love you, but I want to be sure
The only way I can do that, is to be with you more

But Whenever I am with you, time goes by so fast
I have to do all I can, just to make sure that it last

When I'm in your arms it just feels so right
Especially when you hold me, and squeeze me real tight

So I'll savor every moment that I spend with you

Donnie Jackson

And in time we'll realize if our love is true

I hope you don't mind if I'm taking too long
To make sure that together is where we belong

Who Is She

She was just a regular girl, nothing special about her
But she caught my eye, and I knew I had to meet her

At first I resist, I just was not sure
I didn't know who she was, I had to find out more

The first time that I saw her was on Facebook
So I thought; that is where I would start to look

I wanted to see who her friends were
Hoping someone I know knew her

But although she had several friends on there
I didn't know any of them from anywhere

So how will I find out just who she is
I need to know her name, her number, and where she lives

So if you have this information won't you tell me please
I would give anything to find out just who she is

About the Author
Donnie Jackson

Donnie Jackson, the writer of Poetic Love Letters & More, was born on the beautiful island of Jamaica, WI, on December 31, 1955, to Mr. and Mrs. Arthur Jackson. The third of seven children, he has five sisters and one brother. Donnie grew up in Jamaica until the age of eighteen, when he migrated to New Jersey, USA, with his father and five siblings, joining his mother and older sister on July 3, 1974.

Not long after, in November of the same year, he met his wife, Babs. On September 11, 1976, Donnie and Babs got married and have since lived in New Jersey, where they currently reside.

Donnie started writing song lyrics in the early eighties and discovered his passion and talent for writing. He began by crafting a couple of poems, with "It's Not Funny" and "Life" being his first creations. His writing became more frequent and consistent around 2006, inspired by events and situations in his everyday life and the lives of his friends and loved ones.

Acknowledging his gift took time. Donnie initially didn't see himself as a poet, but he eventually recognized his unique ability to create poems from any situation. His friends' encouragement to publish his work led to the creation of Poetic Love Letters & More, a collection of poems that he hopes readers will enjoy as much as he enjoyed writing them.

Milton Keynes UK
Ingram Content Group UK Ltd.
UKHW041830131124
451149UK00001B/250